Maryam Ibrahim holds a Bachelor's Degree in Industrial Engineering from Qatar University. She is currently working as a Planning Engineer in Doha and has been participating in publishing scientific reports. She is a mother to three boys, with whom she shares her love of literature.

MARYAM IBRAHIM

I'M NEVER ALONE

AUSTIN MACAULEY PUBLISHERS®

LONDON ★ CAMBRIDGE ★ NEW YORK ★ SHARJAH

To the apples of my eye:
Khalifa, Ibrahim, and Rashid

"Hi!"
This is me."

"Do you want to know what is special about me?"

"First, He created me as a baby in my mommy's belly."

الْخَالِقُ، الْمُصَوِّرُ، الْمُبْدِعُ

"He is watching over my whole life."
"He saw me fall off my bike."
"It hurt a lot, but I knew that Allah will heal me."
"I knew he can make the hurt go away."
الشَّافِي

"He taught my mom to hug me tightly whenever I am scared.
I always feel safe in her arms."
الرَّحْمَنُ، الرَّحِيمُ، اللَّطِيفُ، الرَّؤُوفُ، الْوَدُودُ

"Allah filled the world with
all kinds of beauty.
With everything we might
need."

الرَّازِقُ، الرَّزَّاقُ، الْوَهَّابُ

الْقَوِيُّ، الْمَتِينُ، الْكَبِيرُ، الصَّمَدُ

"He loves me, and I love him."
الْوَدُود

"He was always there, and always will be .. Till the end of time."
الْأَوَّلُ وَالْآخَرُ

"Watching over me."
"As I try my best to be a
good Muslim."

الرَّقيبُ،العَليم

"My biggest wish is to see him in Jannah."
"The most beautiful place he's created for us."
الْكَرِيمُ، الْمُعْطِي، الْمُتَفَضِّلُ

"I will always
love Allah.
And his love will
never leave me
feeling alone."

The End